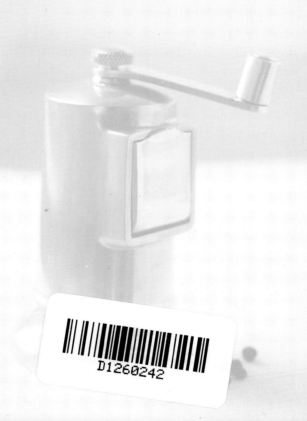

D1260242

CHIC
SIMPLE ®
Components

"I can't cook. I use a smoke alarm as a timer."

CAROL SISKIND

CHIC
SIMPLE ®
Components

COOKING TOOLS

ALFRED A. KNOPF   NEW YORK 1996

THIS IS A BORZOI BOOK
PUBLISHED BY ALFRED A. KNOPF, INC.

Copyright © 1996 by Chic Simple,
a partnership of
A Stonework, Ltd., and Kim Johnson Gross, Inc.

KIM JOHNSON GROSS   JEFF STONE

WRITTEN BY CHERYL MERSER
PHOTOGRAPHS BY GENTL & HYERS
ILLUSTRATIONS BY GREGORY NEMEC
FOOD STYLING BY GEORGIA DOWNARD
STYLED BY AYESHA PATEL

ART DIRECTION BY WAYNE WOLF

Grateful acknowledgment is made to the following for permission to reprint
previously published material:

Doubleday: Excerpts and adapted recipe "Vegetarian Stir-fry" from *Martin Yan,
The Chinese Chef* by Martin Yan, copyright © 1986 by Yan Can & Company, Inc.
Reprinted by permission of Doubleday, a division of
Bantam Doubleday Dell Publishing Group, Inc.

The Pillsbury Company: Excerpt from Pillsbury ad. Reprinted courtesy of
The Pillsbury Company.

Library of Congress Cataloging-in-Publication Data
Gross, Kim Johnson.
Cooking Tools/[written by Kim Johnson Gross, Jeff Stone, Cheryl Merser].
p. cm. — (Chic simple)
ISBN 0-679-44579-X
1. Kitchen utensils. I. Stone, Jeff, 1953–. II. Merser, Cheryl.
III. Title. IV. Series.
TX656.G73 1996
683'.82 — dc20
95-43367
CIP

Printed and bound in Canada
First Edition

"The more you know, the less you need."

AUSTRALIAN ABORIGINAL SAYING

CONTENTS

IN THE BEGINNING

Cutting, carving, grating, shredding, mashing, mincing, and generally changing the shape of food: how to do it and what to do it with. "Victory Garden" chef, Marian Morash.

11

IN THE THICK OF IT

In the stove and on it, what to use, when to use it, what you need to get ready to cook. Diana Shaw on (almost) vegetarian cooking, "First Lady of Desserts," Maida Heatter, and Martin Yan taking the wok mainstream.

33

FIRST AID

Lists of the basic kitchen must-haves, storing, care, and materials, plus a glossary and simply delicious recipes.

84

WHERE

The places to find both what you really need and what you irrationally covet.

93

IN THE BEGINNING

A loaf of bread, a glass of wine, and thou . . . but what happens when you want to cut the bread and open the wine? The right tools reinforce the romance—gliding through bread, easing out a cork. Tasks inspire tools and tools complete tasks. Proficient cooks keep it pure, versatile, comfortable to handle, easy to clean. That way, the food sings, the chef takes a bow, and the tools themselves—a culinary chorus line—stand ready for the next performance.

PERSONAL TOOLS

TOUCH *Kneading (dough), squeezing (fruit juices), rubbing (meats), tearing (greens), measuring (a pinch, a handful), testing (feeling for ripeness).* SIGHT *Inspecting (for bruises, for ripeness), doneness (browning), alarm (smoke, excessive charring).* SMELL *Alarm (burning, spoilage), rewarding (sweet/savory aromas).* SOUND *Freshness (thumping melons), doneness (beeping timers, whistling kettles, popping corn).* TASTE *Seasoning, spoilage, delight—sampling results.*

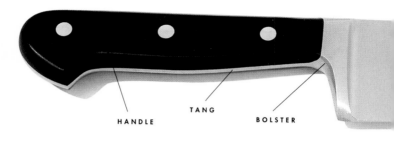

HANDLE **TANG** **BOLSTER**

First Tool. In the Middle Ages, dinners were B.Y.O.K.—bring your own knife. Knives of expensive bronze and plentiful iron had been around for thousands of years, but the 17th century saw the mass production and fine-honing of cutting and carving tools. When buying a knife today, consider the blade, the tang, and the handle.

HANDLE The handle—wood, plastic, or rubber—can either cover the tang or be riveted to it. Let your hand be the judge. **TANG** The tang is the extension of the blade into the handle; in general, the longer the tang, the better weighted the knife. **BOLSTER** The bolster keeps the hand away from the carving area and stabilizes the blade while cutting. **BLADE** Stamped blades are die-cut on an assembly line, while forged blades are shaped and sharpened with greater care, making them more flexible and better balanced. Carbon-steel blades stay sharper but have been all but edged out of the market by high-carbon stainless steel, which may not remain quite as sharp but has compensating virtues: it won't discolor, rust, or abrade.

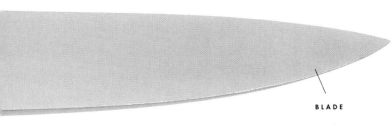

BLADE

8" CHEF'S KNIFE For all-purpose chopping; creating long, thin, julienne strips; dicing small squares of onion; carving roasts in a pinch; and generally making big pieces of food smaller. The chef's knife is wielded by keeping the tip of the blade on the cutting board and rocking the handle up and down in an arc over what you're chopping.

8" SERRATED Treat them as disposable. Serrated blades don't keep an edge, so it's better to buy cheap ones. They're best for foods whose inside is softer than the outside (bread, ripe tomatoes, lush citrus); use them for slicing, not chopping.

4" PARING Essentially a chef's knife, but smaller. Some cooks prefer it for mincing parsley, garlic, or shallots. This is the tool for peeling a cucumber, scraping away a ring of potato skin (and coring out the eye), and cutting items literally under the thumb.

[🐛 FIRST AID—*page 85*]

*Sharp knives are safer;
dull knives slip.
Sharpening has to be an
every-time-you-use-the-knife
ritual to maintain the
edge. Sharpen by holding
the blade at a 15–30°
angle to the rod and
drawing the blade across a
few times on each side.
Even great knives need
grindings from time to
time; go to a hardware
store or butcher for help.*

C A R V E D

**THE MOTION IS A SMOOTH
SLICE, NOT A STACCATO CHOP,
AND THE SHARPER THE CARVING
KNIFE, THE CLEANER THE SLICE.**
1. After cooking and before carving, let the meat or the poultry rest on a warmed cutting board, lightly covered with a piece of foil. A turkey needs 30 minutes, chickens 10 to 20, depending on size. A butterflied leg of lamb should sit for about 15 minutes. 2. Always anchor the meat comfortably with a carving fork. 3. Slice ham with a ham knife straight up and down, other red meats against the grain. 4. If you're serving on a metal platter, warm it first. 5. If you're making your carving debut at Thanksgiving, practice ahead of time on a chicken.

STEP 1. Facing a side of the bird, cavity right, breast left, spear the thigh with your fork, then slice away the thigh and drumstick and remove from the body.

STEP 2. On a separate platter (more room to maneuver), carve the dark meat from the drumstick into even slices.

STEP 3. Pierce the bird with the fork, just above the wing, to secure it. Now cut through the breast parallel to the platter.

STEP 4. Starting mid-breast, carve from the top of the bird down in straight, even slices, until you reach the initial "sideways cut," which will free the slices for serving.

Cutting Boards. A "shambles" is actually a butcher's chopping block, and anything else that's called a shambles (like a teenager's room) resembles a real butcher's block at the end of the day. Despite debates over safety, **WOOD**—easy on both hands and knives—remains safe for routine chopping and carving. Blocks and boards come with different cleaning instructions, depending on the wood's hardness; in any case, clean them well immediately after preparing raw chicken. For carving at the table, a wooden board, with a lip to catch juices, has centuries of ceremony behind it. For preparatory chopping, **POLYETHYLENE** is also highly recommended; indeed, it is specified for industrial use.

CARVING SET

A carving knife is thinner-bladed and more flexible than a chef's knife. A carving fork has curved prongs or a straight "bayonet" to steady the meat—and distance the carver from the blade. (In a pinch, a standard fork can be used.) Bolsters, which are becoming obsolete, shield the hands and allow for resting the tools on the platter. The level of decoration depends on your level of table-side ceremony.

CUTTING BOARD WITH LIP

M A R I A N

BEST KNOWN AS "CHEF MARIAN" ON THE LONG-RUNNING PBS SERIES "THE VICTORY GARDEN," MARIAN MORASH HAS ALSO BEEN A CHEF FOR THE NANTUCKET restaurant she co-founded. She has written several successful cookbooks, using her gift for original vegetable preparation to bring side dishes onto center stage. The victories she's after in the kitchen are those of taste, diversity, and presentation. Lucky for us she always wins.

" NEVER LEAVES HOME WITHOUT Every year we rent a house while my husband works on location for his show 'This Old House.' Every time the agent tells us, 'Oh we know you like to cook, the kitchen's really well equipped!' and you arrive and no pot has a bottom thicker than a dime. My husband won't let me take my kitchen with me but I won't go without the following: • A Zyliss salad spinner • Pepper and (separate) salt grinders; I put the salt on the table and because you can see how much you're actually putting on your food, I'm convinced we're using less. • Paring, chef's, and 12" serrated knives. • A Le Creuset pot with a thick bottom—so my soups won't burn • 12" sauté pan—the sloped sides confine the food to the center of the pan, like a wok, and make it easier to flip ingredients. **FAVORITE UNNECESSARY TOOL** Olive pitters are completely uncritical for a well-stocked kitchen but they really work and I really love olives—for tapenades, Greek salads, and stews—and it's almost impossible to find my favorite kinds unpitted. Doing it by hand is such a mess and you mangle the olive while you're pinching it. Cutting out the pit is tedious. I buy pitters constantly so I won't be without one. **"**

M O R A S H

SWISS CHARD

Swiss chard is one of my year-round all-time favorites. This recipe also works well for broccoli rabe, another favorite.

EQUIPMENT

paring knife
cutting board
large nonaluminum-lined
  saucepan or pot
colander
12" nonstick sauté pan

INGREDIENTS

$1\frac{1}{2}$ lbs. red Swiss chard
2–3 tablespoons fruity olive oil
1–2 tablespoons balsamic vinegar
salt and freshly ground pepper

1. Wash the Swiss chard and separate the stems from the leaves. Cut the stems diagonally into $\frac{1}{2}$-inch-long pieces and tear the leaves into large pieces.

2. Bring a large pot of water to a boil. If the stems are thick, drop them into the boiling water first, and after the water returns to a boil, cook the stems for 2–3 minutes, then add the leaves. If the stems are young and small, place the stems and leaves in the water at the same time.

3. Boil the leaves for 4–5 minutes until they have wilted and the stems are tender. Drain the Swiss chard in a colander and run cold water over it until it is completely cooled. Set aside to drain. (Makes about 6 cups).

4. Heat 2–3 tablespoons of olive coil in a wide, nonaluminum-lined sauté pan and stir in the Swiss chard.

5. Cook, stirring, just long enough to evaporate any excess moisture in the pan and to heat the chard completely. Season with balsamic vinegar, salt, and freshly ground pepper.

"Surrounded by garden overabundance, I fought back by cooking, cooking, cooking."

GRAPEFRUIT KNIF

Specialty Blades. Precise as jewel-cutting instruments, task-specific knives are kitchen collectibles. With a boning knife, chicken or duck breasts peel off a carcass virtually intact, and a blade-weighted cleaver separates serious cuts of meat from the bone. There are "niche" knives for filleting fish, slicing ham, cutting cake, shucking clams, and opening chestnuts. The mezzaluna, a half moon with knobs, performs chopping tasks quickly. The TV ads that scream about the Veg-O-Matic slicer are actually offering a variation on the classic mandoline, which slices potatoes, cucumbers, cabbages, zucchini; you "play" it as if it were a mandolin, in a strumming motion that actually makes arduous tasks calming.

FRUIT KNIVES

Grapefruit knives (above left and opposite) fit the fruit like a glove, their curved blades sliding through pith to release the juicy flesh. They work on all citrus fruits; with practice, they can evenly release melon from its rind. With one thrust, the corer (above right) cores apples and pears cleanly, in seconds.

Blade Runner. It's no coincidence that the last decade's pesto fixation developed with the arrival of the food processor, a device touted as time-saving that actually does save time. Processors, which use centrifugal force to draw in, chop, and spew out, come with discs for slicing thick, slicing thin, or grating. But forget about the discs and go right for the blades. Fitted with the proper blades, the food processor kneads dough, purées soups and vegetables (except potatoes, which become gluey), makes hummus, grates cheese, and whips mayonnaise. As for size, the designers got it right the first time. The standard-size models do more than the minis and do it better than the giants.

Cinema Cuisine

Babette's Feast   THE COOK, THE THIEF, HIS WIFE AND HER LOVER
Delicatessen   DINER   *Eat Drink Man Woman*   EATING RAOUL
Five Easy Pieces   THE WEDDING BANQUET   *La Grande Bouffe*
TOM JONES   *Monty Python's The Meaning of Life*   GANDHI
Like Water for Chocolate   TAMPOPO   *My Dinner with André*   9½ WEEKS
Who Is Killing the Great Chefs of Europe?

THE ESSENTIAL BLADE

The metal blade can process and pulverize anything in a pulsating second, and the plastic blade, otherwise fairly useless, can whip egg whites to fluff up a sorbet.

COUNTERPOINT

In sight, in mind. Here's one tool that will earn its keep within countertop reach. If you put it away, it'll take longer every time to dig out than it will to do the job.

Cuisinart
CLASSIC™

ON •
OFF •
PULSE •

Zesty Tools. Among the easiest and most stylish flourishes any cook (or bartender) can create are pure strips of citrus zest. The only way to make them evenly and consistently is with a citrus zester, like the model shown here. With the sharpened circles against the fruit, pull the zester toward you with one hand while holding the orange, lemon, or grapefruit in the other. You can also "zest" carrots, radishes, and horseradish, making shavings to decorate the tops of salads or vegetable dishes. When making Key lime pie, lemon meringue pie, or gremolata, the zester is a tool that can revolutionize your attitude.

ERGONOMICS

How a tool does its trick is one thing; how it feels in your hand while doing it is ergonomics, *the science of designing devices to function comfortably. An ergonomically correct peeler (above) has a thick, cushioned handle, making it more pleasant and effective to use—especially for those afflicted with arthritis.*

ESTER

"What happens to the hole when the cheese is gone?"

BERTOLT BRECHT

FOUR-SIDED GRATE

Grating. Day-old bread need never go to waste with an easy-to-clean, multi-purpose grater; just grate the bread into crumbs and freeze them. Match the finer teeth to harder ingredients: grate Parmesan, create a dusting of nutmeg, zest a lemon. Coarser grates are better for shredding softer foods like mozzarella, grating potatoes for pancakes, carrots for cake, or zucchini for beignets. The wide-mouthed slicer side makes perfect shavings of Parmesan for salads or cheddar for topping nachos; it also makes vegetables into uniform, disk-like rounds. For bistro flair, use a rotary grater, which makes light work out of shredding chocolate.

GRATE FULLY

Freshly grated cheese and freshly ground pepper are more than restaurant pageantry: The flavors are stronger and the newly released aromas enhance the meal. Choose a **PEPPERMILL** *that grinds coarse (for peppery crusts) or fine (delicate sauces) and loads easily (the one below uses the laundry-chute principle).*

Green Genes. Better oils, new vinegars, and myriad greens have spirited us into new salad days. Reinvented for a health- and ingredient-conscious age, the salad has come into its own, as a separate course or composed to create the meal itself. Vary the drill. To a simple salad add herbs, thinly sliced fennel, peppers, daikon, red onion or scallions, or hard-boiled eggs. Use up leftover vegetables, meats, and fish. Consider olives, nuts, and seeds. Add more stuff, compose it, and turn the salad course into a complete meal. One to three is the vinegar-to-oil ratio. Let your imagination measure the rest. Serve cheese and fruit on the side.

SALAD SPINNER

TOSSING & TURNING

- Drying wet greens: salad spinner or clean pillowcase
- Tearing greens: fingers
- Slicing/julienning vegetables: chef's knife and cutting board
- Preparing garlic: chef's knife or garlic press
- Peeling carrots/ making shavings: vegetable peeler
- Mincing herbs: chef's knife or scissors
- Mixing dressing: whisk, fork, or jar with lid
- Tossing & serving: long-handled salad tongs and bowl with high sides

Handling Pressure. Tools for the culinary equivalent of ironing look unprepossessing, but "smoothing out" food and transforming its textures are gentle and painstaking processes. As arcane as these gadgets may look, they're straightforward. Confront a garlic press with a clove of garlic and the tool will know what to do. You just wield it.

ROLLING PIN When it comes to pastry dough, under- rather than over-roll; flatten a blob of dough only to shape it. A marble pin is cool to the touch, so the dough doesn't get warm as fast, or sticky. And it's heavy, so it does more of the job with its own weight. **GARLIC PRESS** With an action like an engine's piston, the press forces garlic (no need to peel) through tiny holes, releasing flesh and essence. Contrary to myth, pressed garlic isn't more bitter than minced; it's just stronger, so use less. No press? With the heel of your hand, push the flat side of a chef's knife against a clove and the peel will slip right off, leaving the clove ready to mince. **POTATO MASHER** Crisscross the mashing motion for potatoes, and also such other root vegetables as celeriac and parsnips. If mashed foods are popular at your house, consider the French mouli, which removes skins as it mills the food. **MEAT TENDERIZER** Use mostly the flat side, for pounding scaloppine, or beef or tuna for wafer-thin carpaccio. Make a sandwich—wax paper on the outside, meat inside—and pound away. Trim odd bits with scissors for uniformity. Pounding with the waffled side breaks down tough connective tissue in lesser cuts, such as cube steak.

ROLLING PIN

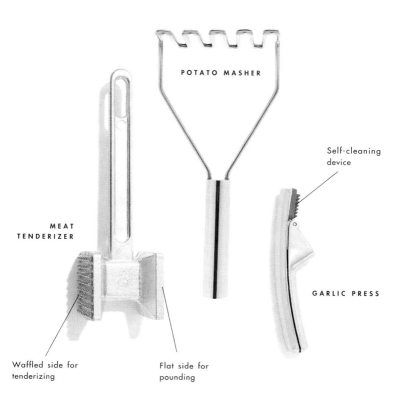

POTATO MASHER

Self-cleaning
device

MEAT
TENDERIZER

GARLIC PRESS

Waffled side for
tenderizing

Flat side for
pounding

IN THE THICK OF IT

Out of the frying pan, into the fire. Measure a little, modify a lot, and adjust the seasoning again at the very end, after the flavors have cooked and blended and mellowed. The challenge of cooking is its immediacy; putting together the elements of a meal is like a puzzle. Prep is perfunctory, but when flavors and textures come together, cooking becomes choreography. And the aim is to take every recipe and make it your own.

> "It is an unwritten law that people who don't cook and who do not savor food own the finest and most fabulously equipped kitchens. . . ."
>
> PAT CONROY, *Beach Music*

Hot Flash. The heat is on. Not only that, it's also in, out, over, under, through, and around. **GAS BURNERS** are superior. The heat is there when you need it, absolutely absent when you don't, and it can be regulated more easily. Gas can go lower than the lowest electric setting. **ELECTRIC OVENS** heat faster, and with less heat fluctuation during cooking. A case can be made for either gas or electric broiling (top heat) or grilling (bottom heat). Given a choice, though, go for the top-of-stove virtues of gas. Professionals always do. **CONVECTION OVENS** do a fabulous job of cooking by using a fan to keep the hot air circulating and the oven at exactly the right temperature. In the process they use less energy (and cause less mess). On a smaller scale, **TOASTER OVENS** can also make bagels, muffins, and baguettes into toast, hold potatoes for baking, and brown the top of a tuna melt. And at countertop level, through the glass door, you can watch.

> "I hate vegetarians. They're so hypocritical.
> At least meat has a chance to run."
>
> RICK DUCCOMAN

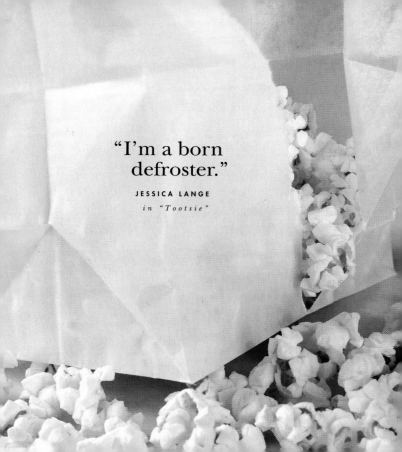

"I'm a born
defroster."

JESSICA LANGE

in "Tootsie"

Zapping. While it hasn't eliminated the conventional oven, the microwave oven has transformed the cooking experience, and the good cooks who still disdain it are usually those who haven't tried it. Microwaves zap the food at its core and cook by working their way back out. (That's why food won't brown in a microwave oven; for browning to occur, heat must penetrate from the outside—in.) Microwaving thaws frozen foods. It also melts (butter, cheese, chocolate). It reheats. It cooks vegetables quickly and with a minimal loss of nutrients. Cooking with microwave energy is unconventional: You can't cook food in metal containers, but plastic, Pyrex, or anything labeled microwave-safe is acceptable. It allows you to cook right on the plate instead of in a pot. Use plastic wrap to seal what's being cooked. (Be sure the wrap doesn't touch the food.)

MICROWAVE 101 BY JULIA CHILD **1.** *Reheating your coffee.* **2.** *Casseroles (they take a fraction of the time).* **3.** *Drying out a damp newspaper (the trick is to keep watching it so it won't catch fire).* **ENHANCING POPCORN** *After popping is finished, throw your choice of toppings into the bag, shake vigorously, and serve. Our all-time favorites are:* • *Grated cheese* • *Herbs* • *Cajun spices* • *Grated chocolate* • *Warm olive oil and mashed garlic* • *Brown sugar melted in butter* • *Kosher salt and freshly ground pepper* • *Tabasco sauce*

D I A N A

IS THE CHEF FOR THOSE OF US WHO "HARDLY EVER" EAT RED MEAT, AND AIM FOR NOURISHMENT WHILE RELISHING FLAVOR. AN AUTODIDACT HOME CHEF, the ever-practical Shaw started writing her food column for the Los Angeles *Times* to help out with her exorbitant entertaining expenses, then grew impassioned. *Almost Vegetarian* is her newest "primer," which shows how delicious real-life, healthy cuisine for part-time vegetarians can be.

"SIMPLEST LOW-FAT COOKING METHOD Steaming is the least you can do to food and still call it cooked. I prefer the collapsible steaming basket, but it's easy enough to make your own steamer with a colander or strainer over a pot: suspend the colander or strainer by its handle (which will stick out over the pot's edge), make sure the water level is two inches below, and put on a lid. **FAVORITE TOOL** Handheld immersion blender. I adore it for puréeing right in the pot: you don't scald yourself while transferring ingredients to the food processor or blender and you have fewer things to clean up. When my house burned down a year ago I went behind a police barricade to salvage this tool—the plastic casing was a little melted but otherwise it still works fine. **CHOPPING CLEAN-UP** Rip open a standard brown paper bag from the grocery store, and lay it over your cutting board. When you're finished chopping, it's easy to pick up all the refuse (peels and skins) and throw it away without having to wash the board again before chopping something else. **"**

S   H   A   W

FAKE POACHING

EQUIPMENT

Microwave-safe high-sided dish or casserole large enough for fish and ingredients

Microwave-safe plastic wrap

Microwave

INGREDIENTS

Fish of choice

Seasonings of choice: broth, white wine, leeks, herbs, lemon juice, etc.

1. Place fish with ingredients in dish. Cover with plastic wrap.

2. Microwave until a knife sinks easily into the thickest part of the fish and some moisture seeps toward the insertion, about 3–4 minutes. The color of the flesh at the deepest part should be opaque, not hard white.

LOW-FAT SAUCES

If you cook your food carefully, it should remain moist enough not to require much sauce, but here are some ways to enhance your meal's flavor:

- For thickeners: Use evaporated skim milk, rice flour, or oat flour; the oat flour has an especially rich, almost buttery flavor
- Flavored vinegars
- Vegetarian broth, thickened with a flour or cornstarch
- Liquid from soaking dried mushrooms
- Meat juices (use a fat-separating pitcher)
- Puréed fresh and dried fruits (soak dried fruits first)

"Cooking well isn't complicated. It takes only three things: appetite, enthusiasm, and good ingredients."

On the Rack. Flavor in, fat out, essence intact. Judiciously mingling fruits, vegetables, potatoes, and meats over a rack for a slow burn seals in the food's flavor while any fat drains away. You can roll, score, stuff, or marinate. You can baste with a metal baster (plastic might melt), test with a meat thermometer, and truss with skewers (or white string).

PAN WITH FLAT RACK

FAT SEPARATOR

ROASTING PAN Essential criteria: Buy sturdy but light—aluminum or stainless steel—because roasts are heavy and spills are a danger. For the same reason, choose riveted handles, not floppy ones. Line the pan with aluminum foil before use—clean-up will be easy. And remember that the pan should fit the oven, not the roast. **FLAT RACKS** Flat racks enable you to pile on more things to roast at once, and can also do double-duty for cooling dessert foods like cakes and cookies. **FAT SEPARATOR** Fat rises, so let it. Just pour the savory stock or pan juices out, and leave the floating fat behind. For better value, buy tempered glass rather than plastic, which can melt. You'll never have to hassle with skimming again.

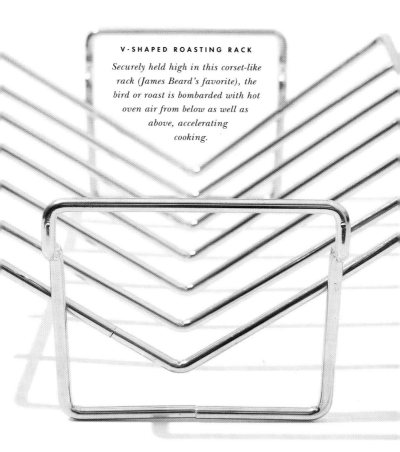

V-SHAPED ROASTING RACK

Securely held high in this corset-like rack (James Beard's favorite), the bird or roast is bombarded with hot oven air from below as well as above, accelerating cooking.

P I Z Z A

PADDLE

To retrieve bread or pizza from the oven the way they do in pizzerias, use the paddle; it's slim, light, and has beveled edges, easy to slide under the pizza and draw it out intact. Easy on, easy off: Dust lightly with flour before sliding pizza on, then brush the flour off the pizza before serving.

STONE

The ceramic pizza "stone" looks primitive, but holds and distributes heat from its porous surface, circulating air and making pizza crust (or flatbread or focaccia) crisper. Or use a cookie sheet, though the crust might not be as crisp.

WHEEL

Some things call for a gesture, and cutting pizza (or focaccia) is definitely one of them. If you're going to the trouble of making it, use a wheel to cut it. Check the wheel to see if it's smooth, and choose the biggest one (probably four inches) you can find.

[*see* RECIPES—*page 88*]

PIZZA ON STONE

DRY MEASURING CUPS

TEMPERED-GLASS MEASURING (

SCALE

"Promises and pie crust are made to be broken."

JONATHAN SWIFT

Measure for Measure. Creative cooks sometimes wing it, but baking is all about precision. Heavier-duty metal tools are more stable than the flimsier versions, preventing spills. **DRY** To measure exactly, pile dry ingredients into a metal measuring cup or spoon, then scrape off the excess with the flat back of a knife blade. **WET** Transparency lets you gauge the exact amount of liquid. Rest cup on a level surface when measuring. Tempered glass can go right into the microwave oven for melting. **WEIGHING** A quarter of a pound? The scale is the best way to tell. An essential for any member of Weight Watchers, the scale outperforms the eye. And children love it for their important tasks—like weighing Play-Doh sculptures.

SURFACE TENSION
Nonstick silicone on aluminum allows you to use less grease and makes removing baked goods foolproof. A springform pan releases cheesecakes and tarts you can't turn over; a loaf pan also makes pound cake; choose muffin tins according to the muffin size you prefer. A cookie sheet with sides will catch drippings from a springform (or any other) pan; one without sides makes it easier to slide crispy cookies off.

3" RAMEK

Ovenware. Brazier, casserole, terrine—ovenware is a vast category, but only as big as you need it to be. One nine-quart casserole with a lid will serve for most dishes; the time to add ramekins is when you want to master individual chocolate soufflés. Ovenware should be heavy enough to conduct and transfer heat, and the same weight on bottom, sides, and top; for all-around use, there should be a cover. Comfortable, sturdy handles are essential (some pots can weigh 15 pounds before you put anything in them). For simple stove-to-table serving (you may want to protect your table with a trivet), ovenware should be attractive enough to be part of the picture.

DUTCH OVEN

Any heavy pot with a lid qualifies; the name's origin is obscure. Thick cast-iron sides guarantee uniform, slow cooking for tough cuts of meat and for braising whole chickens in the oven. It also works well on the range for risotto or for reducing foods that require lengthy simmering (apple or tomato sauce, soups). The enamel prevents rust and makes cleaning easier.

"Nothin' says lovin' like somethin' from the oven."
PILLSBURY AD SLOGAN

[*see* RECIPES—*page 88*]

STANDING MIXER

In the Mix.
When you're about to mix it up, consider the possibilities: combining, beating, blending, churning, frothing, whipping . . . once you settle on the verb, you'll know the best tool for the job.

WIRE WHISK The sturdiest are made from stainless-steel wires welded to a metal handle. "Sauce" or "piano wire" whisks are pear-shaped, and used to beat eggs, or to blend or froth up sauces. So-called "balloon" whisks are bulbous, made of nine or more flexible wires, and used for whipping heavy cream or egg whites. **ELECTRIC BEATER** Convenient models are cordless, lightweight, have detachable arms (for easy cleaning), and should rest on their heels. In a fraction of manual-labor time, you can whip up egg whites, sauces, or a cake; the hardiest models will even mix cookie dough and whip potatoes. **STANDING MIXER** With multiple attachments (juicer, dough hook, etc.), it's easy to justify the counter space. Here you want substantial and heavy—like the classic KitchenAid, which weighs 25 pounds—so it won't vibrate or travel on the job. Standing alone, it can do anything a hand-held electric can, but it relieves the chef's arms and frees her hands.

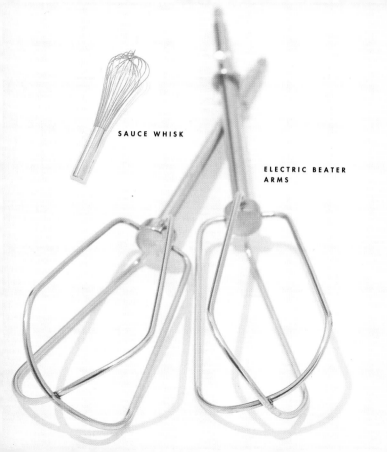

SAUCE WHISK

ELECTRIC BEATER
ARMS

M A I D A

IS ONE OF THE MOST BELOVED "FOODIES" IN AMERICA,

AND NO WONDER: HER DESSERTS HAVE CRISSCROSSED

THE COUNTRY THROUGH HER CLASSES AND IN MORE THAN

a half dozen prized and passed-around cookbooks. Heatter's creations

have been featured at many four-star restaurants and even presiden-

tial lunches, rightly earning her the title of our "First Lady of Desserts."

"BEST WAY TO STORE COOKIES AND OTHER BAKED GOODS Forget the cute cookie jars—because they're not airtight, crisp cookies will get soggy, and moist cookies will get dry. Store in airtight plastic containers—they can also go into the freezer. **BEST WAY TO DEFROST BAKED GOODS** Don't unwrap or open a container until baked goods are completely defrosted; as cakes and cookies defrost, exposed surfaces will sweat, and if the baked goods are directly exposed to air, they will get damp; if left wrapped, the moisture will condense on the outside of the packaging. • If you want to defrost part of a cake, slice off what you need, reseal the packaging, and refreeze the remainder; rewrap the portion you want to defrost so that it can defrost within the wrapping. **FAVORITE MIXING BOWLS** Stainless steel, the larger the better, for mixing and folding in ingredients. Glass is awkward because when the bowl is large, it becomes too heavy for me to stand and hold with one hand while mixing with the other. • Sides should be flared, not vertical—again, this makes mixing and folding easier and avoids making a mess. **"**

HEATTER

CHOCOLATE CHIP PEANUT BUTTER BARS

EQUIPMENT

Baking pan, 9" x 13" x 2"
Food processor
Standing mixer
Mixing spoon
Rubber spatula
Long-bladed knife
Sifter

INGREDIENTS

1 cup salted peanuts
½ cup granulated sugar
1 cup sifted unbleached flour
1 teaspoon baking powder
⅛ teaspoon salt
¾ stick unsalted butter
1 teaspoon vanilla extract
1 tablespoon any jam, jelly, or marmalade
½ cup smooth or chunky peanut butter
¾ packed cup light or dark brown sugar
2 large eggs
2 cups milk chocolate chips

1. Adjust a rack to the center of the oven and preheat to 350° F.

2. Place the peanuts and granulated sugar in the bowl of a food processor fitted with the metal chopping blade. Pulse the machine several times to chop the peanuts. Set aside.

3. Sift together the flour, baking powder, and salt; set aside. In the large bowl of an electric mixer, beat the butter, vanilla, and jam, jelly, or marmalade to mix. Add the peanut butter and beat to mix. Then beat in the brown sugar. Add the eggs and beat until smooth. On low speed beat in the sifted dry ingredients.

4. Remove the bowl from the mixer and stir in the chopped peanuts and granulated sugar. Stir in the chocolate chips.

5. Turn the mixture into the prepared pan, scraping the sides of the bowl with a rubber spatula. Smooth the top and bake for about 35 minutes, reversing the pan front to back once during baking, until a toothpick gently inserted comes out clean.

6. Remove from the oven and let stand until cool. Let stand a few hours or chill briefly until firm enough to cut with a long, sharp knife.

SET OF NESTED BOWL

Bowled Over. The more bowls you have, the more you'll use. Bowls with lips are easier to handle and easier to cover with plastic wrap for storage or zapping. **CERAMIC** is not only pretty for serving but also ovenproof. Unlined **COPPER** bowls are single-use items: when chilled (they conduct temperature better than any other metal) they will jump-start any whipping process. **STAINLESS-STEEL** bowls are lightweight and durable, and a boon in larger sizes for holding enough batter for a double batch of cookies. **TEMPERED GLASS** may not be the most decorative material, but it's neutral enough for table use, tough enough for microwaving and freezers, and its transparency lets you see what you're doing. Because nesting bowls fit within one another when empty, they won't crowd your cabinet. The mini can serve up a few olives while the largest is perfect for salads.

ELECTRIC BLENDE

Vroom. The soul of an old machine, the kind that used to make lovely rich frappés or milkshakes and now makes more restrained smoothies of yogurt and fruit. By day, that is. At night, nothing makes a margarita better. It also pays its rent by liquefying soups, creating light batters, and whipping up "faux" hollandaises, real mayonnaise, and other smooth sauces. It will often work better than a food processor when making bread crumbs or grinding nuts fine. You need only two settings: off and on. Cooked vegetables combined with a little stock, or cooked fruits with cinnamon, creates instant blender babyfood.

SMOOTH SIMPLE

A low-fat shake that's a treat at any meal: Throw into an electric blender your favorite fresh or frozen fruits, some crushed ice, some fruit juice, some nonfat yogurt, and flip the switch. (Of course, you can always add some ice cream....)

*Antifreezing properties
inside this hollow, low-
sided scoop melt the ice
cream or sorbet just
enough so you can
effortlessly form perfect
balls every time.*

Spooning. Spoons for the table nest in the flatware drawer, but spoons for cooking are best kept close at hand in an earthenware crock. For durability, the handle and bowl of a cooking spoon should be one piece, not welded together. **METAL** spoons can stir, scrape the bottom of pots, and serve without staining or burning, but they're not for nonstick finishes. **LADLES** dip, measure, and serve. **WOODEN** spoons are the least technologically advanced material, but they work well with nonstick pans, won't melt if left to rest briefly against a skillet, and are naturally insulated. They're preferable to plastic utensils. **SLOTTED** spoons separate solids from liquids.

TASTING

LADLE

WOODEN

SLOTTED

This wire-mesh basket comes in various sizes and models. Seek out the ones with "ears" because you can rest them atop a bowl or pot while you strain or drain.

The Hole Story. So many strainers, so little storage space. Separating solids from liquids in all amounts is frequently called for in the kitchen, and strainers range from tiny (for tea) to huge (colanders for draining pasta and potatoes). Fine strainers allow you to remove lumps from a sauce or berry seeds from a purée. A few will do.

COLANDER

SIFTER

VEGETABLE STEAMER

COLANDER Models with a sturdy upstanding base are safest, and stainless steel won't discolor. **SIFTER** Use it for sifting and mixing all dry ingredients when baking, but keep it dry or you'll be sifting glue. Instead of sprinkling, sift a perfect dusting of confectioners' sugar over a chocolate cake. **VEGETABLE STEAMER** To steam, the lid goes on top of the pot of boiling water and the steamer insert, preferably one with collapsible sides to fit inside a variety of pots, goes inside. Water underneath, vegetables spread around. Steam until a sharp paring knife slides right through the vegetable, then lift out the steamer, drain, and serve.

Free Range. The big business of pots and pans is an alchemist's triumph: Dozens of alloys are combined to make dozens of pots (two handles, one on each side) and pans (one long handle), each promising what only the cook can really deliver. If you lose the lid, a one-size-fits-all lid will be a more useful long-term investment than you think. A **NONSTICK** sauté pan, for example, will do light jobs with just a trace of oil, while a heavy-bottomed, top-of-the-line, all-purpose saucepan can withstand high-heat reductions. **COPPER** looks great and cooks great, but who's going to keep it shiny? Stockpots for light use (pasta) can be **ALUMINUM**, but if you make a lot of stock, buy heavier ones so food won't "catch" on the bottom. A seasoned **CAST-IRON** skillet takes very high heat and retains it, is great for light frying, and does double duty in the oven. If the handle gets hot, try a plastic slip.

WHAT IS TEFLON? *Though the term is often used inaccurately for a variety of brands, Teflon is the best-known brand name for polytetrafluoroethylene, a nonstick surface coating for almost any kind of pot or pan. The tiniest bit of oil is all you need, so whatever you cook will be that much lower in fat. Use wood, plastic, or nylon spoons and spatulas to avoid scratching the surface.*

[FIRST AID—*page 86*]

N-QUART STOCKPOT

THE STOCKPOT

Use it to slow-simmer soups and stock, stews, and ragouts; for poaching fish and boiling pasta; and, with a colander insert, for steaming. Weight and cost are a judgment call, but make sure the bottom is heavier than the sides or your soups will burn. **RELATIVES** *dutch oven • poachers • doufeu • bean pot • rondeau • pasta pot • couscoussier • vegetable steamer • asparagus steamer • potato steamer*

THE SKILLET

Sloped sides enable you to slide in a spatula with ease, while vertical sides hold up to a sauce and contain sloppy foods like scrambled eggs. Wide and shallow aids evaporation; higher sides hold more. Lids allow for greater flexibility. Heavy metal for the all-around basic skillet ensures good heat conduction.

RELATIVES *omelette pan • crêpe pan • flat griddle • oval pan— for whole fish • blini pan • chestnut pan—with holes in the bottom to allow for direct cooking over heat*

Sized small to melt butter, medium to heat a can of soup, or large enough for a party's worth of rice, saucepans are the pans you'll use most. Choose inexpensive—fast-heating—aluminum for simple chores like boiling water for hard-boiled eggs, and splurge on the versatile 2- or 3-quart size—copper if you can, and one with a comfortable handle. **RELATIVES**

bain-marie/double boiler—for heating delicate things • Windsor saucepan—slope-sided saucepan for reducing sauces • milk pot—tall and narrow for heating and frothing milk • butter melter—small saucepan with spout on side for pouring • sugar boiler—for candy making • preserving pan

POT LUCK

M A R T I

LEARNED COOKING EARLY, AT 13, AS AN APPRENTICE
IN A SUCCESSFUL HONG KONG RESTAURANT, AND
HAS BEEN TEACHING IT EVER SINCE. HIS "YAN CAN COOK"
TV series introduced Chinese methods to the home chef and
demonstrated that the wok could do much more than just stir-fry.

❝BEST TOOL FOR STIR-FRYING The metal Chinese spatula, sold with a wok set
or separately, is a multi-purpose long-handled tool that is curved to fit the sloping
sides of the wok. With it, you can quickly scoop up and toss meat and vegetables as
they flash cook. Larger than the Western spatula or long-handled spoon (you can
substitute these if you choose), the Chinese spatula is most compatible with the wok
and does the job most efficiently. **SMOKING** Smoking can be easily accomplished in
a foil-lined wok. The meat should first be partially cooked or steamed. Before
smoking, sprinkle black tea leaves, camphor chips, and brown sugar (uncooked rice is
often used with the mixture for added aroma) over the bottom of the wok. Place the
meat on a rack in the wok, cover, then quickly heat. The smoke will permeate the meat
imparting a robust, smoky flavor. **STEAMING** Pour water into a wok to a depth of 2
inches. Place a bamboo steamer, cake rack, or crisscrossed chopsticks over the water
(not in). Cover with wok lid and bring water to a boil (the bamboo steamer comes
with its own lid). Place the food in a heatproof dish that fits in the steamer or wok.
Cover and maintain heat to keep water boiling. Occasionally check water level by
carefully lifting lid so the steam rises away from you. Add water when necessary. **❞**

VEGETARIAN STIR-FRY

EQUIPMENT

    wide frying pan
    bowls
    spoon
    cutting board
    paring knife
    wok
    Chinese spatula

SAUCE

    2 teaspoons sesame seeds
    $2/3$ cup chicken or vegetarian broth
    2 tablespoons soy sauce
    $1/2$ teaspoon sugar
    2 teaspoons cornstarch mixed with
        1 tablespoon water

INGREDIENTS

6–8 dried black mushrooms
    1 small zucchini
    2 tablespoons vegetable oil
    2 teaspoons minced fresh ginger
    2 cups small broccoli flowerettes
    3 green onions (white parts only)
        cut diagonally into 2-inch pieces
    1 15-oz. can straw mushrooms,
        drained
    1 15-oz. can baby corn, drained
    $1/2$ cup unsalted roasted peanuts or
        cashews

1. In a wide frying pan, toast sesame seeds over medium heat for about 5 minutes or until golden brown, shaking pan frequently. Then place sesame seeds in a bowl and add all remaining sauce ingredients except cornstarch solution; blend well. Set aside.

2. Soak mushrooms in enough warm water to cover for 30 minutes; drain. With a paring knife, cut off and discard stems; thinly slice caps. Set aside. Slice zucchini in half horizontally then cut each half diagonally into $1/4$-inch-thick pieces; set aside.

3. Place a wok or wide frying pan over high heat until hot. Add oil, swirling to coat sides. Add ginger; cook, stirring, until fragrant. Add mushrooms, broccoli, and green onions; stir-fry for 1 minute. Add straw mushrooms and sauce; cook and toss for 2 minutes.

4. Add zucchini and baby corn; cover and cook for 2 to 3 minutes or until vegetables are crisp-tender, stirring occasionally. Add cornstarch solution and cook, stirring, until sauce boils and thickens slightly. Transfer to a serving dish. Sprinkle with nuts and serve hot.

Sssss. Specialty cooking goes mainstream. With a nod to tradition, slightly flattening the wok's bottom means it no longer perches precariously on the stove, and adding a nonstick finish means you cook with less oil. A wok is light, and it cooks fast; you toss and turn the foods—fish, meats, vegetables—or stir the sauces over high heat that distributes itself in a split-second sizzle, keeping tastes, colors, and textures intact. It can also braise, lightly poach (with a lid), and gently sauté when your sauté pan is otherwise engaged. If you want to remain authentic, add a bamboo steamer, a stir-fry spatula, and a strainer. Stir-frying at home is versatile, clean-tasting, fresh, quicker than having it delivered, and the way we eat now. Rice on the side, of course.

> ## "You do not sew with a fork, and I see no reason why you should eat with knitting needles."
>
> MISS PIGGY

FISH SPATULA

Flip Side. Specialized spatulas aren't essential but they make turning, flipping, and lifting a pleasure instead of a risk. The flat part of a spatula is called a blade, and well-made metal ones are sharp enough for cutting, say, a linzer torte into clean halves. Heavy, **SQUARE-TIPPED METAL** blades have beveled edges, the better to scoop up your food. Minimal flexibility provides droppage protection. Plus, they're trustworthy under grilling heat—perfect for burgers. **WOODEN** blades are hard to find but if you see one, grab it. Chefs love that they're naturally insulated and can work for any pan surface. **SLOTTED** spatulas drain as they lift. Fish spatulas scoop up a filet or steak without flaking it and drain away any oil or poaching liquid.

"I only eat red meat that comes from cows that smoke."

DENIS LEARY

CHARCOAL FLUE

This cylinder holds and heats charcoal, keeping the heat intense until the coals are glowing—and ready. Lift the flue by the wooden handle slowly, allowing the preheated coals to spread out into a perfect bed of heat.

Smokin'. The cavemen did it, and no generation since then has seen any reason to stop. Marshmallows over a campfire, a fire-escape hibachi, a grill fueled by charcoal, wood, or propane—the lure is still fire against food. Mixed vegetables brushed with herbed oil lightly browned on each side. Lamb marinated in oil, port wine, and garlic. Fish brushed with a fruit juice–based marinade as it sears. Pork seasoned with peppercorns, oil, and champagne vinegar. Chicken touched gently at the end of its cooking with barbecue sauce. Peaches or apricots fired with a light sprinkling of brown sugar. And steak, sausages, hot dogs, burgers. Bonus: We no longer have to catch it to cook it.

FIRING IT UP

*Longer handles than
usual keep outdoor tools
close to the fire while you
back off. Tongs are
precise outdoors for
turning, but a spatula
is still* de rigueur *for
hamburgers. Keep a
knife outside with
the fork, for testing
doneness.*

PAINT BY NUMBER

*To transfer a bowl of
flavoring to the food
being cooked, use a sauce
brush or paint brush. Not
a slather but a glaze: Less
is definitely more. Spread
the sauce, herbed oil, or
marinade over the top of
the meat (or whatever)
lightly, without quite
touching the edges, so as
not to draw flames up
over the side. Glowing
coals cook, but
flames burn.*

Lift-off. Coffee was actually drunk in Europe in coffeehouses before it was ever brewed in the home; indeed, the quality of a café is still judged by its coffee. "Caff" or decaf; espresso or cappuccino; iced coffee; coffee plunged, infused, pumped, dripped, filtered, or boiled. With dozens of beans and blends to choose from, what coffee we like and how we make it are personal choices, down to the cups, mugs, or demitasse cups we choose to drink it from. This little espresso maker, for example, sends the water up through a shaft to the coffee, then back down as espresso. Certain coffee rules are fixed: Avoid instant coffee; store fresh coffee or beans in the freezer; put used coffee grounds in the compost.

CUPPA JAVA

Clean the pot. • *Freshly ground beans, along with pure, cold water, are all it takes.* • *Use 2 level teaspoons for every 6 ounces of water (or more or less coffee, for stronger or weaker).* • *Drink at once, or reheat in the microwave.* • *Explore the possibilities: cappuccino, caffe latte, exotic beans.*

THE GRIND

Generally, faster processes (espresso) require finer grinds. Below are some general guidelines.

- *Plunger pots: coarse*
- *Most flat-bottom drip makers: medium*
- *Cone-shaped filters: extra fine*
- *Professional-quality espresso machines: "gritty" powder fine*

PRESSO MAKER

Instant Karma. You need a kettle. You need a teapot and a strainer, or at least a cup infuser. You need tea, or tea bags if you must, but that's the least of it—even a few fresh mint leaves steeped in water that's just below the boiling point will create a pot of comforting tea. Don't let the kettle reach a roiling boil. Warm the teapot just as the water boils, then steep the tea, one teaspoon per teacup, for three to five minutes. Here is the handle, either on the side (more English) or the top (more Oriental), and the spout is high up, because tea is strongest on top, and the strongest tea gets poured through the strainer first. English teas tend to stimulate, while Oriental green teas soothe.

ELECTRIC CITRUS JUICER

*A wrist-saving device for the fresh, quick, morning orange or grapefruit juice
and limeade or lemonade. Place the halved citrus, pulp side down, on
the reamer. Pushing down is the tool's signal to juice. Kids love juice
even more if they've made it themselves.*

Juicy Fruit. For the times you need just a little citrus juice, turn
your hands into a manual juicer. Prick half a lemon, lime, or orange
several times with a fork, pressing against the shell; then squeeze.
If you're after even more serious juice—carrot, spinach, beet, celery,
peach, apple, parsley—an electric juice extractor lets you make any
kind, even your own version of V-8 juice. Washed vegetables go in,
skin and all, then go round and round and come out as juice.

For sandwiches. For sealing leftovers in bowls, any kind. For stretching tight over Pyrex or glass before microwaving. The noncling kind really doesn't. Paper bags ripen tomatoes, steam roasted peppers so they're easy to peel, or drain fried chicken or calamari. Despite these various uses, they tend to pile up anyway in the utility closet.

"Cooking tip: Wrap turkey leftovers in aluminum foil and throw away."

NICOLE HOLLANDER

FOILED AGAIN

In olden times it was known as tin foil, but these days aluminum does the foiling. It covers the inside of a pan to keep it clean, and can cover the outside of a pot in place of a lid. It wraps, or double-wraps, over plastic bowls. It makes pouches of things—garlic, fish, mixed and marinated vegetables—for grilling.

BAG IT

A Ziploc bag can hold laundry, wet bathing suits, and toiletries when you're traveling, and school supplies and sortables when you're not. The bag of choice for freezing, especially single-serving ice cubes of frozen chicken stock, homemade pesto, or tomato sauce. Zip open, pull out cubes as needed, and always press out extra air before sealing or resealing.

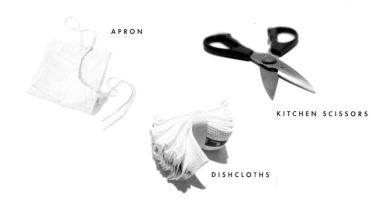

APRON

KITCHEN SCISSORS

DISHCLOTHS

Kitchen Basics. A gimmick might be best defined as an unused gadget. As kitchens grow smaller, tools proliferate; visions of insecure cooks dance in marketers' heads. You don't need a pitter unless pitting olives or making cherry *clafoutis* is an everyday thing in your household. That egg ring can probably wait, too, for another time. These are the unsung heroes: a stack of clean dish towels; your most comfortable shoes; a can opener, an apron (but no toque), a thick baking mitt. And the things that follow on these pages.

BAKING MITT

CAN OPENER

Storage. Good storage keeps food from turning into alarming science experiments. A container with a tight-fitting lid will keep baked goods moist without letting in moisture from outside. Mason jars and well-made canisters are airtight countertop containers. You can hold a Tupperware party right in your own fridge, with leftovers of all sizes, then put them directly into the microwave oven. (Date them with a masking tape label—even the most hermetically sealed leftovers will turn into the most freakish science experiments before you know it.)

Taming of the Screw.

Wine for the table is one thing; wine in the kitchen is quite another. A splash of wine, red or white, enhances a marinade, deglazes pan juices, or makes a sauce complex when reduced at a rolling boil. Wine belongs in risottos, in main-course soups, in the court bouillon you use to poach a fish. Drizzle a little port wine into a wedge of Stilton, and let it sit until the salad's served. And don't forget to toast the chef.

WINGED CORKSCREW Our unofficial survey: Women prefer the winged corkscrew, which, once the worm is in place, does its leveraging with a push on the arms. (You're not supposed to use the tip of the worm to scrape off the metal foil, but most people do anyway.) Men generally prefer the waiter's corkscrew so they can show off and do the leveraging themselves. **WAITER'S CORKSCREW** This compact model is packable, foldable, travel-worthy, and a picnic staple. The penknife is handy for removing a wine bottle's lead foil. The lip folds out, providing the leverage to pull out the cork, and it also opens cans and bottles.

"I drink to make oth

GEORGE

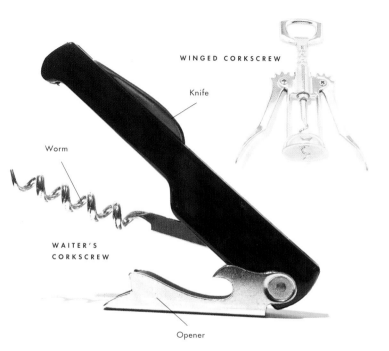

WINGED CORKSCREW

Knife

Worm

WAITER'S
CORKSCREW

Opener

:ople more interesting."

H A N

first aid.

Chefs aren't always being disingenuous when they say all they need to cook are a wooden spoon, a chef's knife, and a sauté pan. Start by buying only what you need for cooking what you like to eat. As you learn more, buy the more exotic—as long as it really makes it easier.

RULES OF THUMB

1. Wash hands before cooking! 2. Keep a fire extinguisher handy in case of kitchen fires. 3. Never throw water on a grease fire. Use salt, baking soda, or, if the area is a small one, a metal lid. 4. When pan-frying or sautéing, keep a colander handy to place over the pan should the fat begin to spatter.

FIRST AID

For a minor cut during food preparation, wash the wound, apply an antiseptic cream, and bandage. For anything more severe, seek medical help.

BASIC KITCHEN MUST-HAVES

- Blender or food processor (a food processor is more versatile)
- Dish scrubbers
- Drying rack
- Fire extinguisher

- Packaging for leftovers: aluminum foil, freezer bags, plastic storage containers, plastic wrap, wax paper
- Oven with stove range, self-cleaning preferred
- Refrigerator with freezer, self-defrosting
- Sponges
- Trash and recycling bins

UTENSILS AND MORE

BASIC NECESSITIES

- Bowls, nested tempered glass or stainless steel
- Can/bottle opener
- Colander, stainless steel
- Corkscrew
- Cutting board, of thick hardwood or acrylic
- Grater, 4-sided stainless steel
- Ladle, 8-ounce

- Measuring cups, 1-cup and 2-cup,
  Pyrex glass
- Pepper grinder, adjustable
- Pot holders
- Potato masher/ricer
- Salad spinner
- Salad tongs
- Spatula, slotted stainless-steel blade
- Spoons, mixing, wood and stainless steel
- Spoons, measuring, heavy-gauge
  stainless steel
- Spoon, slotted
- Strainer, 8-inch
- Vegetable steamer, collapsible
- Whisk, stainless steel

BEYOND NECESSITIES

- Barbecue set, long-handled
- Brush, pastry
- Chimney flue
- Fish spatula
- Juicer, citrus and/or all-purpose
- Garlic press
- Kitchen timer
- Meat pounder/tenderizer
- Salad bowl and serving implements
- Thermometer, oven

BAKING

BASIC NECESSITIES

- Baking sheets, 18 x 12 x $1/2$ inch
- Bowls, nested set in tempered glass
- Loaf pan, 8-inch
- Measuring cups, stainless steel
- Measuring spoons, stainless steel
- Parchment paper

- Rectangular pan, 9 x 12-inch
- Rolling pin
- Rubber spatula
- Sifter
- Square pan, 8-inch
- Wax paper
- Whisk, electric beater, or standing mixer

KNIVES AND BLADES

BASIC NECESSITIES

- Bread knife, serrated 8-inch
- Chef's knife, 8-inch
- Food processor or blender
- Paring knife, 4-inch
- Scissors, utility
- Sharpening steel

BEYOND NECESSITIES

- Apple corer
- Carving set
- Grapefruit knife
- Poultry shears
- Vegetable peeler
- Zester

STORING BLADES

*Never store knives in drawers unless
they're sheathed: Blades that get bumped
get dull. Pros prefer wall-mounted magnetic
strips—easy to see, easy to retrieve. Wooden
blocks are okay, but there's guesswork in
finding the knives each time, for handles
tend to look alike. And never store knives
within reach of children or pets.*

POTS AND FRYING PANS

BASIC NECESSITIES

- Roasting pan, shallow, 15 x 10 x 2 inches
- Roasting rack, flat, stainless steel
- Saucepan, 2-quart, with lid
- Skillet or sauté pan, nonstick, 8-inch, with lid
- Skillet or sauté pan, nonstick, 13-inch, with lid
- Stockpot, 8-quart, heavy-bottomed, with lid

BEYOND NECESSITIES

- Ceramic casserole, with glass lid
- Double boiler / bain-marie
- Dutch oven
- Hot plate: for keeping food hot as part of a buffet
- Kettle
- Skillet, cast-iron, 9-inch: great for frying chicken
- Wok, nonstick

HOW TO CARE FOR A CAST-IRON PAN

When you first purchase a cast-iron pan (or an old one has rusted), scrub it clean with hot water and scouring powder, then rinse and dry completely. Lightly coat it with vegetable oil and place it in a preheated oven at 300° F. for 30 minutes. Rub clean with paper towels. If any evidence of rust appears on the towels, rub pan alternately with salt and towels until the towels come away clean. Rub in a final layer of oil. If possible, after subsequent use, do not wash pan with soap and water; instead, wipe it with a paper towel lightly moistened with water and then with one that has been lightly moistened with vegetable oil.

MATERIAL PROPERTIES

Aluminum. PROS: *It's lightweight and conducts heat well. To prevent warping, buy thickest, heaviest gauge available. Good for most purposes, including poachers, stockpots, roasting, baking, and omelette pans.* CONS: *Acidic foods and juices will stain it and impart a metallic taste to the food. Boiling implements in a weak cream of tartar solution (2 teaspoons powder to 1 quart water) will remove stains.*

Cast Iron. PROS: *Thick, durable, and excellent for heat retention at high temperatures (pan-frying fish or chicken). If the cast iron is enameled (Le Creuset is a popular brand), it achieves almost nonstick qualities of preventing food from sticking and requiring less cooking oil; the enamel also prevents rusting.* CONS: *It's heavy, especially for the weak-wristed; has to be seasoned to prevent sticking; takes some time to get hot; and may rust if you're not careful. The best way to prevent rust is to dry over a hot burner until all droplets of water evaporate.*

Copper. PROS: *It's ideal for conducting heat.* CONS: *It's expensive and requires frequent polishing. Also, because the surface that touches food must be coated with a non-reactive metal (such as stainless steel) to prevent discoloration and the metal tainting the food's flavor, it's hard to tell how much the copper is actually affecting the cooking.*

Earthenware. PROS: *Allows for slow oven baking because it conducts and holds heat well. Reasonably priced whether or not it's glazed.* CONS: *Because it's fragile, it's best to buy smaller shapes. Never plunge hot earthenware into cold water.*

Porcelain. PROS: *Despite its fragile appearance, it can take the heat, even a few seconds under the broiler to brown a crème brûlée. Perfect for soufflé dishes, individual ramekins, gratin dishes, and quiche pans.* CONS: *It can be difficult to clean; follow stoneware cleaning guidelines.*

Stainless Steel. PROS: *It's strong and won't discolor.* CONS: *It doesn't conduct or retain heat well unless mixed with other metals: Aluminum or carbon alloys at the core improve stainless's cooking properties.*

Stoneware. PROS: *It can do anything that earthenware can, but is much more durable.* CONS: *Sensitive to temperature. Soak to remove cooked-on food; scour only with a plastic scouring pad to protect glaze.*

Tempered Glass *(popular brand: Pyrex).* PROS: *It's made to withstand the cold and the heat—be it a freezer, microwave, or traditional oven. Used for pie pans, casseroles (with or without lids), and measuring cups. Easy to clean, inexpensive, and acceptable for the table.* CONS: *Susceptible to radical shifts in temperature. Can be difficult to clean: avoid abrasive scrubs or wire pads that will scratch finish.*

RECIPES

Pesto

EQUIPMENT
Food processor
Salad spinner

INGREDIENTS
1–2 cloves garlic
1 large bunch fresh basil, leaves only
    (washed and dried in salad spinner)
$\frac{1}{4}$ cup pine nuts, pecans, or walnuts
$\frac{3}{4}$ cup grated Parmesan cheese
$\frac{1}{2}$ cup olive oil

1. Place garlic in the bowl of a food processor fitted with a steel blade and chop until fine. Add basil, pine nuts, pecans, or walnuts, and process until fully blended.

2. Add Parmesan cheese to the processor and very, very slowly add olive oil, gradually increasing the amount. **NOTE:** Pesto freezes well and has a refrigerator life of about three days. Be sure to add a thin layer of olive oil on top of pesto before storing. Pesto can also be frozen in ice-cube trays and then defrosted and used as needed.

Georgia Downard's Individual Chocolate Soufflés

EQUIPMENT
- Electric mixer
- Saucepan
- Whisk
- 6 individual ramekins (1-cup)

INGREDIENTS
- 4   egg yolks
- $1/2$ cup sugar
- $1/3$ cup flour
- 2   cups milk, heated
- 5   ounces semi-sweet chocolate, melted
- 6   egg whites
- confectioners' sugar for garnish
- Butter for greasing ramekins

1. Preheat the oven to 425° F. In a bowl with an electric mixer, beat the egg yolks with $1/4$ cup of the sugar until mixture ribbons. Beat in the flour and milk. Transfer to a saucepan and cook over moderately low heat, whisking, until the mixture is thickened. Do not boil. Stir in the chocolate.

2. In another bowl, use the electric mixer to whisk the whites until they form soft peaks. Add the remaining $1/4$ cup sugar and whisk until the whites form stiff peaks. Stir $1/4$ of the whites into the chocolate mixture and fold in the remaining whites. Spoon the mixture into 6 buttered ramekins. Bake for 5 minutes. Reduce heat to 375° F. and continue to bake for 10–12 minutes more, or until puffed and lightly firm to the touch.

Simple Pizza

EQUIPMENT
- Small bowl
- Food thermometer
- Food processor
- Pizza paddle
- Pizza stone or baking sheet
- Grater
- Serrated knife
- Measuring cup
- Measuring spoons
- Marble work surface (preferred)

INGREDIENTS
- 1   package active dry yeast
- $2/3$ cup warm water (110°–115° F.)
- Pinch of sugar
- 2   cups unbleached all-purpose flour
- $1/4$ cup cornmeal
- 1   teaspoon kosher salt
- $1 1/2$ tablespoons olive oil

OPTIONAL INGREDIENT
- $1/2$ cup fresh rosemary, basil, or oregano, or $1/4$ cup dried

TOPPING
- $2 2/3$ cups grated fresh mozzarella cheese (with grater)
- 4   beefsteak tomatoes, thinly sliced (with serrated knife)
- $1/4$ cup chopped fresh basil
- 2   tablespoons dried oregano

PROCESS

1. Place yeast in a small bowl. Stir in the water and the sugar. Let stand for about 10 minutes, then mix. Don't dawdle: The dough gets sticky very quickly and the longer you wait, the more trouble you'll have getting the pizza off the peel. The water used to make pizza dough should be lukewarm—110° F. is ideal. If you have any doubts about the temperature, use a meat thermometer.

2. In a large mixing bowl or work bowl of a food processor, combine flour, cornmeal, optional herb, if desired, and salt. Add yeast and olive oil, and mix well.

3. Set dough mixture on a work surface dusted with flour. Knead dough vigorously for about 5 minutes. Divide dough into 4 equal parts and shape into balls.

4. Lightly oil a baking sheet. Transfer dough onto sheet and lightly brush each ball with olive oil. Cover baking sheet with plastic wrap and let sit in a warm place until dough has doubled in size (about 1½ hours).

5. Dough can be frozen at this point, if desired. Place dough balls in plastic freezer bags and freeze. To defrost, let thaw ompletely at room temperature before rolling out.

6. Preheat oven to 500° F. for at least 20 minutes. If using a pizza stone, place stone in cold oven before heating. Grease a baking sheet. Depending on the size of your baking sheet, you may only be able to fit only 2 pizzas at a time.

7. Flatten dough ball with heel of hand on lightly floured work surface. The smaller the dough ball, the easier it is to work. Lift and pinch each disk from center outward in a circular motion until dough is thin. Don't worry about the occasional holes and don't use more dough than the recommended amount. Wait until you're an expert before making a large pizza: it's easier to manage a smaller amount of dough.

8. Place dough on a pizza paddle, or "peel," that has been liberally sprinkled with cornmeal.

9. Sprinkle 1⅔ cups of the mozzarella evenly among the 4 pizzas. Place tomatoes in a circle on top of the mozzarella, then fill in with more slices. Sprinkle on the remaining mozzarella and the fresh basil or dried oregano.

10. Slide pizza onto the preheated stone that has been just sprinkled with cornmeal by giving a slight, quick jerking movement forward and then backward. Or put it on an oiled baking sheet.

11. Lower heat to 475° F. and cook pizza for 7–10 minutes, or until dough is golden.

glossary.

Terms of the trade tell you what to do with the tools of the trade. Knowledge is power: If you are familiar with the basic terminology, no recipe will seem too difficult. Choose any cuisine and make it yours.

How the Raw Becomes the Cooked

BASTING. Usually associated with meats and poultry, basting involves brushing on or pouring liquid over foods while they are cooking, to keep them moist and flavorful. When basting meat, the basting liquid is usually a combination of pan drippings and fat. Seasonings or other ingredients may be added to enhance taste. The best basting brushes are made of natural boar bristles. Make sure the bristles are securely attached to the handle.

BLANCH. To cook foods—most often vegetables—briefly in boiling water and then set briefly in cold water until completely cool. Food is blanched for one or more of the following reasons: to loosen and remove skin (almonds, peaches, tomatoes); to enhance color and reduce bitterness (for crudités); to extend storage life (raw vegetables to be frozen); to draw out excess salt from meats, such as bacon and salt pork.

BRAISING. To sauté food in either fat (traditionally), beer, wine, broth, juice, or water, then simmer at low heat, in a covered saucepan.

BROILING AND GRILLING. Both cooking methods are quick processes of cooking food close to a very hot heat source. When grilling, you're usually outside (unless you have a stove-top grill), using your barbecue to cook food over glowing charcoals. When broiling, you're indoors, using your oven to cook food under a heat source (a gas oven is better for this than electric coils). Grilling should make meat crisp on the outside and leave it moist inside. The oven or barbecue should be hot before cooking food. When using either method, cook red meat and vegetables 4 inches from heat; chicken or turkey 6–8 inches from heat. Always remove charred areas from food before eating.

DREDGE. To lightly coat moist ingredients with a dusting of powderlike substance (e.g., herbs, spices, flour, cornmeal). Always shake loose any excess coating, as it will cook faster and burn easily.

FRYING VS. SAUTÉING. Frying is a way of cooking food (usually predipped in flour or batter) by submersion in hot oil. Sauté, from the French sauter (to jump), means to rapidly cook small pieces of food over high heat in oil or fat. The Chinese version is called stir-frying; it usually involves less oil and a wok.

GREASE. To coat the interior of a pan with fat to prevent food from sticking.

PREHEATING. Turn on oven to the desired temperature at least 20 minutes before baking, roasting, or grilling, to insure that the oven reaches the desired temperature.

SEAR. To brown food quickly by sautéing in a pan, under a broiler, or on a grill to seal in a food's juices while making the food's exterior pleasantly crisp.

SIMMER. To cook liquid, and anything in it, over a low heat just below the boiling point. Small bubbles may rise to the surface. If left uncovered, the liquid will become concentrated.

STEEP. To allow dry ingredients (tea, dried fruits, sun-dried tomatoes) to sit in warm liquid. In the case of tea, the steeping liquid is the desired product. In the case of dried fruits

and tomatoes, more often than not the liquid is discarded, as its only purpose is to plump things that have become overly desiccated.

How to Cut It

CHIFFONADE. To cut leaves of easily bruised fresh herbs, like basil, by rolling the leaves and then slicing them across into very fine strips.

CHOPPING. To cut food into small, but not necessarily even, pieces. To chop: Hold the blade firmly and bring a large knife up and down all over the material to be chopped.

DICING. To cut into even, tiny cubes. Dicing results in smaller pieces than does chopping but larger than does mincing. Remove a small slice from the bottom of whatever you want to dice, so that it lies flat on the board. Cut the vegetable into sticks, then cut the sticks into cubes. The size of the sticks and how thick you slice them determine the size of the dice.

FILLET. To debone a cut of meat or fish. (As a noun, fillet or filet refers to the meat once its bones have been removed.)

JULIENNE. To cut into fine, even-sized sticks, which are also called matchsticks. These strips are used to garnish soups, stews, and salads, or they can be steamed and served as a side dish.

MINCE. Mince means to chop food very finely. Parsley and garlic are typically minced.

How to Handle Liquids

CURDLE. *Certain foods will separate, or curdle, when heated too rapidly (dairy products are especially susceptible); flour acts as a binding agent to prevent this from happening. If a dish curdles, all is not lost; you can often incorporate the ruined batch into the new.*

DEGLAZE. *To pour liquid—water, stock, wine, or liquor—into a pan in which food has been roasted or sautéed in order to absorb the glaze and the browned, crusty bits formed on the bottom of the pan. These concentrated, coagulated meat essences add wonderful flavor to a dish or sauce.*

DEGREASE. *To skim fat from the surface of a soup or sauce. This can be done with a spoon and additional fat can be absorbed with paper towels. A less labor-intensive solution is to ladle the liquid into a special degreasing pitcher with a trap door at the bottom. Then you can allow the non-fatty meat juices to escape from below, stopping the flow when only the fat remains. If there is time enough to allow the liquid to thoroughly chill, then the fat rises to the top in a semisolid layer that is easily removed.*

GLAZING. *Applying any thick liquid that lends a lustrous coating to food.*

REDUCE. *To heat a liquid to a boil, and leave uncovered and simmering so that liquid will condense in volume and flavor.*

RENDER. *To extract an animal fat from its connective tissue by melting. Two rendered fats used in cooking are chicken fat and lard, which is pork fat. Rendering is a slow process, done in a heavy-bottomed pan over low heat. It continues until all the fat has liquefied, the tissue has turned brown and crispy, and any impurities have sunk to the bottom of the pan. The remaining clear fat is strained carefully through filter paper. The practice of rendering is losing favor among health-conscious cooks.*

SCALD. *To scald milk is to heat it just shy of boiling. To scald solid food is to briefly immerse it into already boiling water.*

> "Ask not what you can do for your country. Ask what's for lunch."
>
> ORSON WELLES

where. From drugstore to designer

boutique, seductive kitchen accoutrements are harder to resist

than to find. Window shop in catalogs. Browse in boutiques.

Practice potential tools by helping out in a friend's kitchen. Keep

a kitchen wish list, then fill it using the reputable sources below.

FREEDOM OF CHOICE

Even as the world shrinks and chain stores expand globally, there are plenty
of locales where choice is limited, if there is any choice at all. However, most
manufacturers today can aid you in finding a store or even mail direct to you.
The numbers listed below will help give you freedom of choice.

MANUFACTURERS

All-Clad	800/ALL-CLAD	Ikea	800/434-4532
Amana	800/843-0304	General Electric	800/626-2000
Bodum	800/232-6386	Kenwood	800/536-9663
Braun	800/272-8610	KitchenAid	800/422-1230
Calphalon	419/666-8700	Krups	800/526-5377
Chantal Cookware	800/365-4354	Le Creuset of America	800/729-0908
Corningware/Revere	800/999-3436	Replacements, Ltd.	800/562-4462
Cuisinart Corp.	800/726-0190	Revere	800/999-3436
Farberware	800/562-4226	Tupperware	800/858-7221

NATIONAL RETAILERS/MAIL-ORDER CATALOGS

BALDUCCI'S
800/225-3822
(Gourmet foods; catalog available)

BED, BATH & BEYOND
212/255-3550
(Kitchen storage items)

BERGDORF GOODMAN
800/967-3788 for catalog
(Tableware)

BLOOMINGDALE'S
800/777-4999 for store catalog
800/777-0000 for Bloomingdale's by Mail Ltd.
(Upscale department store; kitchen- and tableware)

BRIDGE KITCHENWARE
800/274-3435 outside of NYC only
212/688-4220
(Full range of imported, professional kitchenware; catalog available)

CHEF'S CATALOG
800/338-3232
(Professional kitchenware)

CRATE & BARREL
800/323-5461 for catalog information
(Kitchen utensils)

DEAN & DELUCA
800/221-7714 for catalog
212/431-1691 for store
(Gourmet foods and spices, cooking supplies)

DAYTON HUDSON/ MARSHALL FIELD
800/292-2450
(Department store; kitchenware)

DILLARD'S PARK PLAZA
501/661-0053
(Kitchenware, cookware, tableware)

HOME DEPOT
404/433-8211. Call for locations.
(Kitchenware)

IKEA
800/434-4532
(Department store; cookware; catalog available)

JOHNSON BROTHERS BY WEDGWOOD
800/677-7860
(Cookware)

LECHTER'S
800/605-4824
(Kitchenware and utensils)

R. H. MACY & CO., INC. (BULLOCK'S, AÉROPOSTALE)
800/45-MACYS
212/695-4400 for East Coast listings
415/393-3457 for West Coast listings
(Department store)

NORDSTROM
800/285-5800
(Kitchenware, cookware)

PERFEX
800/848-8483
(Peppermills)

POTTERY BARN
800/922-9934 for catalog
(Housewares)

SUR LA TABLE
800/243-0852 for catalog
206/448-2244 for store
(Professional-quality kitchen- and bakeware)

TARGET
612/370-6073 for location nearest you
(Kitchen- and tableware)

TIFFANY & CO.
800/526-0649 for catalog
(Tableware)

WILLIAMS-SONOMA
800/541-2233
(Kitchenware, kitchen storage items)

United States

CALIFORNIA

CAPRICORN GOURMET
COOKWARE
100 Throckmorton Avenue
Mill Valley, CA 94941
415/388-1720
(Gourmet cookware)

COOKING
339 Divisadero Street
San Francisco, CA 94117
415/861-1854
(Nostalgic and professional cooking equipment)

HOMECHEF
3525 California Street
San Francisco, CA 94115
415/668-3191
(Kitchenware and cooking school)

HOME EXPRESS
800/800-0510. Call for locations.
(Chain of home furnishing stores featuring table- and kitchenware)

KITCHEN ART
142 South Robertson Boulevard
Los Angeles, CA 90048
310/271-9499
(Kitchenware)

SWISS KITCHEN
228 Bon Aire Center
Green Brae, CA 94904
415/461-1011
(Kitchenware, cookware)

CONNECTICUT

FOOD FOR THOUGHT
221 Post Road West
Westport, CT 06880
203/226-5233
(Cookware)

THE PANTRY
Titus Road
Washington Depot, CT 06794
203/868-0258
(Cookware, tableware)

THE SILO
44 Upland Road
New Milford, CT 06776
203/355-0300
(Cookware, kitchen appliances, cooking school)

ILLINOIS

ELKAY
MANUFACTURING
COMPANY
2222 Camden Court
Oak Brook, IL 60521
708/574-8484
(Cookware)

ST. CHARLES
MANUFACTURING
COMPANY
1611 East Main Street
St. Charles, IL
708/584-3800
(Cookware)

MICHIGAN

THE KITCHEN PORT
415 North Fifth Avenue
Ann Arbor, MI 48105
313/665-9188
(Cookware, kitchenware)

NEW YORK

ABC CARPET & HOME
888 Broadway
New York, NY 10003
212/473-3000
(Kitchenware, tableware)

AD HOC SOFTWARES
410 West Broadway
New York, NY 10012
212/925-2652
(Kitchenware, tableware)

BROADWAY
PANHANDLER
477 Broome Street
New York, NY 10013
212/966-3434
(Cookware, kitchenware)

CHAMBERS,
GARDENER'S EDEN,
POTTERY BARN,
WILLIAMS-SONOMA
OUTLET
231 Tenth Avenue
New York, NY 10011
212/206–8118
(Tableware)

E.A.T.
1064 Madison Avenue
New York, NY 10028
212/772-0022
(Gourmet foods, kitchenware)

FELISSIMO
10 West 56th Street
New York, NY 10019
212/956-4438
800/708-7690 for catalog
(Serving pieces)

FISHS EDDY
889 Broadway
New York, NY 10003
212/420-9020
*(Hotel, club, and restaurant
tableware)*

GRACIOUS HOME
1220 Third Avenue
New York, NY 10021
212/517-6300
(Kitchenware, tableware)

HENRO
525 Broome Street
New York, NY 10013
212/517-6300
*(Antique kitchen- and
housewares)*

HOPE &WILDER
454 Broome Street
New York, NY 10013
212/966-9010
*(Antique uphostered furniture
and housewares)*

INTÉRIEURS
114 Wooster Street
New York, NY 10012
212/343-0800
(Tableware and furniture)

KITCHEN ARTS &
LETTERS INC.
1435 Lexington Avenue
New York, NY 10128
212/876-5550
*(Authoritative cooking
literature source)*

LAMALLE
KITCHENWARE
36 West 25th Street
New York, NY 10010
212/242-0750
(Kitchenware, tableware)

TAKASHIMAYA
693 Fifth Avenue
New York, NY 10022
212/350-0100
(Tableware)

TARZIAN HOUSEWARES
194 Seventh Avenue
Brooklyn, NY 11215
718/788-4213
(Cookware)

T. SALON
142 Mercer Street
New York, NY 10012
212/925-3700
(Full tea emporium)

WOLFMAN-GOLD & GOOD
116 Greene Street
New York, NY 10012
212/431-1888
(Tableware)

ZABAR'S
2245 Broadway
New York, NY 10024
212/787-2000
(Gourmet foods, kitchenware,
and catering)

ZONA
97 Greene Street
New York, NY 10012
212/925-6750
(Dishware)

OHIO

KITCHEN COLLECTION
71 East Water Street
Chillicothe, OH 45601
614/773-9150
(Kitchenware, appliances)

OREGON

POWELL'S BOOKS FOR
COOKS
3739 SE Hawthorne
Portland, OR 97214
503/235-3802
(Cookbooks and specialty foods)

WASHINGTON

CITY KITCHENS
1527 Fourth Avenue
Seattle, WA 98101
206/382-1138
(Kitchenware and cookware)

INTERNATIONAL
LISTINGS

Great Britain

THE CONRAN SHOP
Michelin House
181 Fulham Road
London SW3
171/589-7401
(Kitchen and tableware)

DAVID MELLOR
4 Sloane Square
London SW1W
171/730-4259
(Kitchen equipment and
tableware)

FORTNUM AND MASON
18 Piccadilly
London W1A 1ER
171/734-8040
(Legendary food hall;
extensive collection of kitchen-
and tableware)

HABITAT UK LTD.
206 King's Road
London SW3
171/351-1211. Call for
branch listing.
(Kitchen and tableware)

HARRODS FOOD HALL
Knightsbridge
London SW1X
171/730-1234
(Gourmet foods, kitchenware)

HEAL'S
196 Tottenham Court Road
London W1A
171/636-1666
(Home accessories)

JERRY'S HOME STORE
163-167 Fulham Road
London SW3 6SN
171/225-2246
(Kitchenware)

MUJI
26 Great Marlborough
Street
London W1V
171/494-1197. Call for
branch listing.
(Special Japanese foods;
selection of cookware and
tableware)

RESOURCES

Any unlisted items are from
private collections.

JACKET FRONT

cast-iron **FRYING PAN**
from a private collection

BACK

GRAPEFRUIT KNIFE by
Wüsthof

COOKING TOOLS

12–13 stainless-steel **CHEF'S,
SERRATED** and **PARING
KNIVES** by Wüsthof

16 antique silver **CARVING
SET** from Hope & Wilder,
NYC

17 wooden **CARVING BOARD**
from a private collection

20–21 **GRAPEFRUIT** and
CORING KNIVES by
Wüsthof

23 **FOOD PROCESSOR** and
CHOPPER BLADE by
Cuisinart from Broadway
Panhandler, NYC

24 **SWIVEL PEELER** by Oxo
Good Grips from Williams-
Sonoma

25 **ZESTER** from Broadway
Panhandler, NYC;

**UNTREATED STEEL TABLE
SURFACE** by Stephen
Schermeyer from Ad Hoc
Softwares, NYC

26 stainless-steel **4-SIDED
GRATER** by Williams-
Sonoma, NYC

27 stainless-steel **PEPPERMILL**
by Perfex from Broadway
Panhandler, NYC

28 **SMALL CANNING JAR**
from Broadway
Panhandler, NYC

29 **SALAD SPINNER** by
Zyliss from Broadway
Panhandler, NYC

30 **ROLLING PIN** by Dean &
Deluca, NYC

31 aluminum **MEAT
TENDERIZER** from
Lamalle Kitchenware, NYC;
stainless-steel **POTATO
MASHER** from Lamalle
Kitchenware, NYC; self-
cleaning **GARLIC PRESS**
by Zyliss from Broadway
Panhandler, NYC

32 cast-iron **FRYING PAN**
from a private collection

40 tempered-glass **FAT
SEPARATOR,** nonstick
ROASTING PAN, and
stainless-steel **FLAT RACK,**

all from Broadway
Panhandler, NYC

41 stainless-steel **V-SHAPED
ROASTING RACK** from
Broadway Panhandler, NYC

42 wooden **PIZZA PADDLES:**
top antique, bottom
Williams-Sonoma; small
ceramic **PIZZA STONE** by
Kitchen Supply Co. from
Broadway Panhandler,
NYC; stainless-steel **PIZZA
CUTTER** from Williams-
Sonoma

44 stainless-steel **MEASURING
CUPS** from Williams-
Sonoma; stainless-steel
MEASURING SPOONS
from Zabar's with
tempered-glass
MEASURING CUP by
Pyrex from Zabar's, NYC ;
WEIGHING SCALE by
Pelouze from Broadway
Panhandler, NYC

45 **NONSTICK BAKING
PANS** from Broadway
Panhandler, NYC

46 **RAMEKIN** (or soufflé cup)
by Apilco from Williams-
Sonoma; linen **NAPKIN** by
Muriel Grateau from
Intérieurs, NYC

47 **DUTCH OVEN** by Le Creuset from Broadway Panhandler, NYC

48 **STANDING MIXER,** by KitchenAid from Broadway Panhandler, NYC

49 stainless-steel **WHISK** from Broadway Panhandler, NYC; **ELECTRIC BEATER ARMS** by KitchenAid from Broadway Panhandler, NYC

52 11-piece set of tempered-glass **NESTED BOWLS** by Duralex from Williams-Sonoma

54 **ELECTRIC BLENDER** by Waring from Broadway Panhandler, NYC

56 **ICE CREAM SCOOP** by Zeroll from Dean & Deluca, NYC

57 **TASTING SPOON** from Broadway Panhandler, NYC; **SLOTTED SPOON** from Williams-Sonoma

58 stainless-steel mesh **STRAINER** with handle by Carlo Gianni from Broadway Panhandler, NYC

59 stainless-steel **COLANDER** from Broadway Panhandler, NYC; stainless-steel **SIFTER** from Dean & Deluca, NYC; stainless-steel **VEGETABLE STEAMER** from Williams-Sonoma

61 10-quart stainless-steel **STOCKPOT** by All-Clad from Broadway Panhandler, NYC

66 nonstick **WOK** and wooden cooking **CHOPSTICKS** from Broadway Panhandler, NYC

68 stainless-steel **SLOTTED FISH SPATULA** from Broadway Panhandler, NYC

69 stainless-steel blade **SOLID SPATULA** from Broadway Panhandler, NYC

70 **CHARCOAL FLUE** by Williams-Sonoma

71 nonstick **BBQ SET** by Charcoal Champion from Lechter's

73 aluminum 3-cup **ESPRESSO MAKER** by Bialetti from Dean & Deluca, NYC

74 **IRON KETTLE** from the office of Chic Simple; **TRAY** and **BAMBOO SCOOP** from T. Salon, NYC; hotel-silver **SPOON** from Henro, NYC

75 tempered-glass **TEAPOT** by Bodum, stainless-steel **KETTLE** by Revere, **MESH TEA BALL**, and **TEA STRAINER**, all from Broadway Panhandler, NYC; **TEA BAG** from T. Salon, NYC

76 **CITRUS JUICER** by Braun from Broadway Panhandler, NYC

78 tempered-glass **BOWL** (part of 11-piece set) by Duralex from Williams-Sonoma

79 aluminum **BAKING TRAY** (under raspberries) from Lamalle Kitchenware, NYC

80 **APRON** from Bed, Bath & Beyond, NYC; waffle-weave cotton **DISH TOWELS** from Williams-Sonoma; **KITCHEN SCISSORS** from Broadway Panhandler, NYC

81 **BAKING MITT** from Zabar's, NYC; **CAN OPENER** by Zyliss from Zabar's, NYC

83 stainless-steel **WINGED CORKSCREW** by Wüsthof; **WAITER'S CORKSCREW** from Zabar's, NYC

QUOTES

2 **CAROL SISKIND,** from *Just Joking,* edited by Ronald L. Smith and Jon Winokur (Word Star International, 1992).

6 **AUSTRALIAN ABORIGINAL SAYING**

18 **MARIAN MORASH,** as told to Chic Simple, 1995.

19 **MARIAN MORASH,** from *The Victory Garden Cookbook* (Knopf, 1982). Recipe adapted from *The Victory Garden Fish and Vegetable Cookbook* (Knopf, 1993).

26 **BERTOLT BRECHT,** from *Peter's Quotations: Ideas for Our Times,* edited by Laurence J. Peter (Quill/William Morrow, 1992).

33 **PAT CONROY,** *Beach Music* (Doubleday, 1995).

34 **RICK DUCCOMAN,** *The Montreeal Comedy Fest/Juste Pour Rire* (Performance, July 1989).

36 **JESSICA LANGE,** in *Tootsie* (1982).

37 **JULIA CHILD,** as told to Chic Simple, 1995.

38 **DIANA SHAW,** as told to Chic Simple, 1995.

39 **DIANA SHAW,** from *Almost Vegetarian* (Clarkson Potter, 1995). Recipe as told to Chic Simple, 1995.

44 **JONATHAN SWIFT,** from *A Cultured Glutton: A Collection of Literary Quotes,* edited by John Goode (Headline Book Publishing, 1987).

47 **PILLSBURY AD SLOGAN**

50 **MAIDA HEATTER,** as told to Chic Simple, 1995.

51 **MAIDA HEATTER,** recipe adapted from *Maida Heatter's Brand-New Book of Great Cookies* (Random House, 1995).

64–5 **MARTIN YAN,** quote and recipe adapted from *Martin Yan, The Chinese Chef* (Doubleday, 1985).

67 **MISS PIGGY,** from *The Penguin Dictionary of Modern Humorous Quotations,* edited by Fred Metcalf (Penguin, 1988).

69 **DENIS LEARY,** "No Cure for Cancer" (*People* magazine, May 24, 1993).

78 **NICOLE HOLLANDER,** from *The Fifth and Far Finer than the First Four 637 Best Things Ever Said ,* edited by Robert Byrne (Ballantine Books, 1993).

82–3 **GEORGE JEAN NATHAN,** from *1,911 Best Things Anyone Ever Said,* edited by Robert Byrne (Ballantine Books, 1988).

92 **ORSON WELLES,** on reaching 300 pounds, from *The Fourth and By Far the Most Recent 637 Best Things Anybody Ever Said,* edited by Robert Byrne (Ballantine Books, 1991).

101 **DAVE BARRY,** from *The Taming of the Screw* (Rodale Press, 1983).

104 **ESCOFFIER,** meaning "Make it simple," from *A Food Lover's Companion,* edited by S. Herbst (Harper & Row, 1979).

VOICES

MAIDA HEATTER

Maida Heatter's Brand-New Book of Great Cookies (Random House, 1995); *Maida Heatter's Greatest Dessert Book Ever* (Random House, 1990); *Maida Heatter's Book of Great American Desserts* (Knopf, 1985); *Maida Heatter's New Book of Great Desserts* (Knopf, 1982); *Maida Heatter's Book of Great Chocolate Desserts* (Knopf, 1980); *Maida Heatter's Book of Great Cookies* (Knopf, 1977); *Maida Heatter's Book of Great Desserts* (Knopf, 1974)

MARIAN MORASH

The Victory Garden Fish and Vegetable Cookbook (Knopf, 1993); *The Victory Garden Recipes; From the Garden to the Table* (video/book distributed by Knopf, 1987); *The Victory Garden Cookbook* (Knopf, 1982)

DIANA SHAW

Almost Vegetarian (Clarkson Potter, 1995); *Grilling from the Garden* (Harmony Books, 1993); *Sweet Basil, Garlic, Tomatoes, and Chives* (Harmony Books, 1992); *Vegetarian Entertaining* (Harmony Books, 1991)

MARTIN YAN

Martin Yan's Culinary Journey Through China (KQED Books, 1995); *A Simple Guide to Chinese Ingredients and Other Asian Specialties* (Yan Can Cook, 1994); *The Well-Seasoned Wok* (Harlow & Ratner, 1993); *Everybody's Wokking* (Harlow & Ratner, 1991); *A Wok for All Seasons* (Doubleday, 1988); *Martin Yan, The Chinese Chef* (Doubleday, 1985); *The Yan Can Cookbook* (Doubleday, 1981); *Yan Can & So Can You* (Doubleday, 1981); *The Joy of Wokking* (Doubleday, 1979)

INVALUABLE RESOURCES: *The Cooks' Catalogue,* James Beard, Milton Glaser, Burton Wolf, et al., eds. (Avon, 1977); *The Well-Tooled Kitchen,* Fred Bridge and Jean F. Tibbetts (Hearst Books, 1991)

"Today, people tend to take tools for granted. If you're ever walking down the street and you notice some people who look particularly smug, the odds are they are taking tools for granted."

DAVE BARRY

CHIC SIMPLE STAFF

PARTNERS Kim & Jeff
ASSOCIATE EDITOR Victoria C. Rowan
ART DIRECTOR Wayne Wolf
ASSOCIATE ART DIRECTOR Alicia Yin Cheng
OFFICE MANAGER Joanne Harrison

ACKNOWLEDGMENTS

COPY EDITOR: Borden Elniff **SPECIAL THANKS TO:** The James Beard Foundation, Paul Bogaards, Claire Bradley, Erica Cantley, Amy Capen, Julia Child, Tony Chirico, Jill Cohen, Henry Daas, Anne Diaz, Edward Kemper Design, Jane Friedman, Janice Goldklang, Katherine Hourigan, Andy Hughes, Madhur Jaffrey, Carol Janeway, Gia Kim, Nicholas Latimer, William Loverd, Anne McCormick, Dwyer McIntosh, Sonny Mehta, Anne Messitte, Eberhard Müller, The New School Culinary Arts Program, Phillip Patrick, Takuyo Takahashi, Suzanne Smith, Anne-Lise Spitzer, Jeffrey Steingarten, Shelley Wanger, Amy Zenn.

COMMUNICATIONS

Thanks for all the letters, postcards, e-mail, faxes, and occasional manuscript in a bottle that washes up to our studio. Your observations and suggestions are welcomed and immensely helpful. Since a lot of the questions we get are about what else is in the Chic Simple book series or what's coming next, we created a catalogue. If you would like to receive one for FREE, please send us a set of icing-covered (preferably chocolate) beaters, or just your address to:

CHIC SIMPLE
84 WOOSTER STREET • NEW YORK, NY 10012
fax (212)343-9678
E-mail address: info@chicsimple.com
Compuserve number: 72704,2346
Website address:
http://www.chicsimple.com

Stay in touch because "The more you know, the less you need."

HARDWARE

Power PC 8100, Apple Macintosh Quadra 700 and 800 personal computers; APS Technologies Syquest Drives; Iomega Zip Drive; MicroNet DAT Drive; SuperMac 21" Color Monitor; Radius PrecisionColor Display/20; Radius 24X series Video Board; Hewlett-Packard LaserJet 4, Supra Fax Modem; provided and maintained by Abacus Solutions, New York, New York.

SOFTWARE

QuarkXPress 3.3, Adobe Photoshop 2.5.1, Microsoft Word 5.1, FileMaker Pro 2.0, Adobe Illustrator 5.0.1

MUSICWARE

Greg Brown (*The Live One*), Art Pepper Meets the Latin Rhythm Section, The Best of James Bond, Mary Chapin Carpenter (*Stones in the Road*), Cyrus Chesnut (*Revelation*), John Coltrane (*Soul Train Blue Train*), Desperado (*Motion Picture Soundtrack*), The Subdudes, Ingrid Lucia & The Flying Nutrinos (*I'd Rather Be in New Orleans*), Friends of Dean Martinez (*The Shadow of Your Smile*), French Kiss (*Motion Picture Soundtrack*), Grateful Dead (*Hundred Year Hall*), Emily Harris (*Wrecking Ball*), Billie Holiday (*Solitude* and *Lady in Autumn/The Best of the Verve Years*), Chris Issak (*Forever Blue*), It's a Beautiful Day (*It's a Beautiful Day*), Joy of Cooking (*American Originals*), k. d. lang (*All You Can Eat*), Los Lobos (*La Pistola y El Corazón*), Hugo Montenegro & His Orchestra (*Music from "The Good, the Bad, and the Ugly"*), Morphine (*Cure for Pain*), Nusrat Fateh Ali Khan (*Mustt Mustt*), Zbigniew Preisner (*Bleu*).

TYPE

The text of this book was set in two typefaces: New Baskerville and Futura. The ITC version of **NEW BASKERVILLE** is called Baskerville, which itself is a facsimile reproduction of types cast from molds made by John Baskerville (1706–1775) from his designs. Baskerville's original face was one of the forerunners of the type style known to printers as the "modern face"—a "modern" of the period A.D. 1800. **FUTURA** was produced in 1928 by Paul Renner (1878–1956), former director of the Munich School of Design, for the Bauer Type Foundry. Futura is simple in design and wonderfully restful in reading. It has been widely used in advertising because of its even, modern appearance in mass and its harmony with a great variety of other modern types.

SEPARATION AND FILM PREPARATION BY

COLOR SYSTEMS, INC.
New Britain, Connecticut

PRINTED AND BOUND BY

FRIESEN PRINTERS
Altona, Manitoba, Canada

CHIC SIMPLE LIBRARY

Also available in the Chic Simple series:

**BODY   CLOTHES   COOKING
HOME   WOMEN'S WARDROBE**

and in Chic Simple Components:

**BATH BED LINENS DESK
EYEGLASSES   NURSERY PACKING
PAINT SCARVES SCENTS SHIRT AND TIE
STORAGE TOOLS**

Forthcoming Spring 1996:
CHIC SIMPLE ACCESSORIES

"Faites simple."

ESCOFFIER